D1624822

# TRADITIONAL
# IRISH LAWS

▼

Mary Dowling Daley
Illustrated by Ian McCullough

APPLETREE PRESS

First published in 1997 by
The Appletree Press Ltd, 19-21 Alfred Street,
Belfast, BT2 8DL
Tel:  ++44 (0)1232 243074
Fax:  ++44 (0) 1232 246756
email: frontdesk@appletree.ie
Copyright © Mary Dowling Daley, 1997
Illustrations © Ian McCullough, 1997

Traditional Irish Laws

A catalogue record for this book is available from The British
Library.

**website: www.irelandseye.com**

ISBN 0-86281-685-8

9 8 7 6 5 4 3 2 1

# Introduction

The ancient laws of Ireland were promulgated by the pagan Celts who arrived in Ireland over two thousand years ago. They began to arrive as early as 500BC and were well established a century before the birth of Christ. The Celts dominated the island for nearly a thousand years, resisting challenges and absorbing influences from other cultures for many centuries more.

They emerged as a recognisable people in the area which is today northern Germany, Austria, and Bohemia, and spread across Europe as far east as the Ukraine and as far west as the Irish Sea and the Atlantic Ocean. They spread over much of France in the sixth century before Christ, invaded northern Spain in the fifth century, burned Rome in 390BC, and destroyed stoa at Athens in 279BC. Their conquests and rampages across Europe were referred to by Hecateus of Miletus at the end of the sixth century BC and by the Greek historian Herodotus in the fifth century BC.

Despite their warlike ways, the first century AD historian Strabo wrote that the Celtic druids were "the most just of men". These wise men were the judges and advocates of ancient Ireland. In the sixth century AD, almost one thousand years after arriving in Ireland, Irish Law scholars first wrote down the pagan Irish laws. Until then, it had been taboo for them to put their sacred laws into writing.

As they rampaged their way across Europe, the warrior Celts poached customs observed by various members of the Indo-European language family and introduced a system of law which defined social and cultural codes. These customs included the caste system of India; fosterage or training by relatives in a hereditary career such as king, warrior, poet, public buffoon or charioteer; Germanic fines for assault and murder instead of prison; the use of satire, ridicule and invective to enforce the law; distraint of livestock as a way of forcing arbitration between a wrongdoer and a victim; respect for women; and respect for domestic animals.

Ireland, unlike the rest of mainland Europe, avoided Roman conquest, and the Irish system of law remained unique, in effect a living museum of primitive Indo-European customs. The first serious threat to the continuity of the old pagan laws was the enactment of the Statutes of Kilkenny in 1366, two hundred years after the Anglo Norman conquest of Ireland.

The Norman colonists who settled in Ireland were culturally disparate. Settlement in Ireland was fragmented and some settlers went native, adopting Irish customs, speech and Irish names. The Statutes banned intermarriage with the native Irish, prohibited land-leasing with them, and outlawed Irish dress and fosterage. These laws were an effort by the conquerors to Anglicise the settlers and protect them from Irish influences.

The Statutes of Kilkenny did not succeed in anglicising the settlers as attested by the following English Statute passed in 1537, during the reign of Henry VIII:

" ...ther (sic) is ... nothing which doth more conteyn and

keep many of his subjects of this his said land, in a certaine savage and wild kind and manner of living, then the diversitie which is betwixt in tongue, language, order and habite."

During the reign of Queen Elizabeth I, 1558-1603, the ancient laws were banned and the manuscripts hidden. The manuscripts were buried or hidden behind loose stones in the hearth. P J Dowling's account in *The Hedge Schools of Ireland* (London 1933) describes how manuscripts kept by rural old men became "so black with smoke, and so tattered and old" that it was impossible to read them. Other manuscripts have been lost to hungry mice or torn apart by children. Fortunately several of the manuscripts have survived, and are now held in Trinity College, Dublin and the British Museum, London. Written in Irish by the pagan, wise druids, these precious manuscripts are a testimony to an ancient, influential people and their system of law.

# Animals

*It is no disgrace for a chieftain of the highest grade to have a pet hog, a greyhound, a calf and a lap dog with his wife.*

❦

*The hen's trespasses in the house: snatching food, spilling grain from a sack and leaving her droppings behind. The law is the same for pet herons, pet cranes and old pet hawks.*

❦

*It is illegal to overide a horse, force a weakened ox to do excessive work or threaten an animal with angry vehemence which breaks bones.*

*There are three trespasses of a hen in a herb garden: the soft-swallowing of bees, injury to the dye-plants, and attacks on the garlic. A guilty hen shall have her feet tied together, or rag boots put on.*

❧

*If a trespass is committed by the dog that herds cows, the dung-hill dog that guards the house, the lap-dog or the greyhound that live inside with the family, let a plank be placed across the dog's feeding trough and let the culprit not be fed.*

❧

*The following shall be tied or attended so they do not commit assault: the springing dog, the dog with whelps, a crouching dog and a dog, against which searching does not avail.*

*Cows and bulls are exempt from liability for charging at humans during cattle-bulling season.*

❦

*If the cat in the kitchen attacks a member of the family, but it was in the work of mousing she did it, she is exempt from liability.*

# Assemblies

❦

*If grass on the hill of the great assembly has not grown back since the previous meeting, cloths are to be spread under kings and rushes under the inferior grades of Irish.*

❦

*If a king of Leinster neglects preparations for his great assembly he shall suffer early greyness, baldness, or feebleness.*

*Book of Leinster*

*All arms must be laid aside: all grudges,*
*feuds, and quarreling are illegal.*

❦

*Debtors who attend the great assembly may not*
*be pressed for payment of debts.*

*If you ride your chariot to the great assembly and it is damaged, you may not claim compensation unless it was broken through furious driving.*

❧

*Horses that collide on the king's racecourse are exempt from liability, for racing is their proper work at the time of the great assembly.*

❧

*At the main feast of the assembly the king and the chief poet of the tribe shall be served a thigh of the roast. The young lord is served a leg. Blacksmiths and charioteers shall be served the head and queens get haunches.*

# Barter/Property

*The wife who minds the sheep shall be
paid two lambs a year.*

❧

*The builder of large cook-houses, that is, kitchens
for the free public hostel, earns six cows.*

❧

*To rent six cows from your chieftain for one year the fee
is one live calf, one slaughtered pig preserved with salt,
three sacks of malt to make ale, half a sack of wheat,
and a handful of rush candles.*

*The* builder of ships earns four cows a year.

❧

*Before* you send malt to the chief, test a grain of it against

your tooth lest the ale he brew be bitter or mawkish.

*The builder of causeways, that is, stepping stones across a river, earns two cows a year, as does the builder of chariots, or huts of timber and mud.*

❦

*The chief poet of the tribe earns twenty-one cows annually, plus enough pasture lands to feed them, plus two hounds and two horses.*

❦

*The overseer of the poor and the wretched earns one cow of second quality.*

*The king of a territory earns one cow and a salted
pig for his help in making a treaty between the tribes.*

❦

*In fords and wild places, one leap of the bull is free to
the cow's owner, provided no arrangements were made
beforehand.  If the meeting was arranged, the owner of the
bull may claim every fourth calf that resembles its sire.*

# Battle

❦

*Seven places where battle is not permitted: in the sanctuary of a church, adjacent to a church, in the court of a king or on his lawn, in the house of every chieftain of the noble grades, and on the lawn of a hostel-keeper or a poet.*

❦

*These are the occurrences which would postpone every battle: the arrival of a king; a bishop or a chief poet; the death of thy father, thy mother or thy wife.*

*In the case of the woman-battle where one woman wishes to recover a debt, both must first raise their distaffs (from which thread is drawn in spinning) and their comb-bags (the bags of wool they keep at their feet while spinning) in the presence of their guardians. They must always fast first. It is illegal to conduct this battle on the king's lawn.*

❦

*There is a fine for stripping the slain soldier of his jewels but it is not unlawful to strip the slain deserter.*

*Cases of bloodshed where the physician receives*
*only half the total of the fines to be paid:*
* *a wound in battle or contest of enmity;*
* *the blood of a man escaping from the battlefield;*
* *the blood of a man who draws his sword upon anyone;*
* *blood shed on a rock; or*
* *blood shed by falling from a tree.*

*The man who sheds blood is conveyed over the bloody sod:*
*the noble chiefs protect him from the rush of the crowd.*
*If he is a noble chariot warrior he is carried on the*
*shoulders of his men; his chariot is brought along with him.*

*Eriu XII*

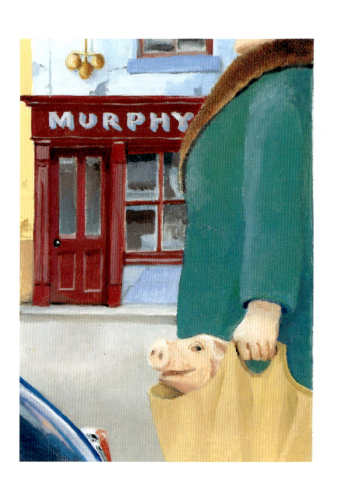

# Borrowing, Lending and Bad Debts

❦

*A wife may give items of minor value as pledges against a loan,
such as clothing, personal effects, pigs and sheep, without the
permission of her husband.  But she may not pledge a cow,
a horse, gold, silver, copper or iron against her husband's wishes.*

❦

*If a person who is of a higher rank than you refuses to
repay his debt you may sit at his doorstep and fast until
he submits to arbitration.  If you die before he submits he
shall be blamed for your death and shall suffer lifelong disgrace.*

*If* the owner of a boat is absent you may not
take his boat out in a storm (unless danger lurks.)

❧

*W*hen fleeing from an enemy you may borrow a horse,
a weapon, or a boat without permission of the owner.

❧

*S*even pledges there are which are of little value and need
not be accepted as collateral for a loan:

• a chessboard;

• a beautiful tooth (that is, the tooth of a whale or a wild animal);

• the eyebrow of a whale;

• a child's first playthings, (little cats and dogs too young to work);

• a chained dog, too vicious to be useful;

• a horse that will not pull a chariot or allow a man on its back; or

• an oxen that will not plough.

## Caste and Honour

🍎

*The fine for unjustly satirising the young lord who owns seven cows, seven pigs, and seven sheep is the same as for burning down his house or for violating his daughter.*

*Four dignitaries whose status in society may be downgraded:*

- *a false-judging king;*
- *a stumbling bishop;*
- *a fraudulent poet; and*
- *an unworthy chieftain.*

❦

*The Aire Echtai: a chief of five men equipped for war whom he keeps near him in time of peace to avenge and punish all insults (particularly violence by murder) done to his tribe.*

❦

*A king shall be downgraded to the status of commoner if he is found at the handle of an axe or a spade, or pounding turf with a mallet. Or if the back of his head is injured while fleeing the battlefield.*

# Children and Fosterage

❦

*For each to his task has been appointed:*

*Let the farmer's son go to the land.*

*The king's son to bind hostages.*

*Let the carpenter's son follow the adze,*

*to fashion a board aright;*

*Let the smith's son take to coal - 'tis*

*his due to follow in the calling of his family.*

*Let the trumpeter's son carry the trumpet,*

*the harpist's son a harp.*

*Let the physician's son become a leech.*

*Let the poet's son take to poesy,*

*the buffoon's son to sharp satires.*

*Let the judge's son be without decadence, so that*

*the judgment from his lips may reach everybody.*

*Irish poem, 8th century; Eriu, Volume IX*

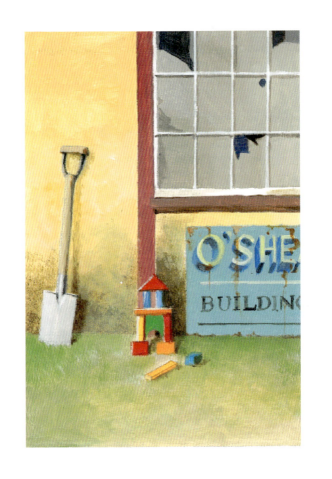

*Whether the offspring of kings, warriors, poets,
workers in wood or stone, or tillers of the soil, a son
or daughter shall follow the career of his or her parents.*

❦

*A foster child shall live with a distant relative in the tribe while
being trained in a hereditary career and shall return to birth
parents at marriage age: fourteen for girls, seventeen for boys.*

❦

*A black cradle coverlet and a black tunic shall be given
to the foster mother when the child is given to be fostered,
the coverlet without being threadbare, and the tunic
without being broken whether these be given with the child
of a person of high or inferior rank. A skillet and a cow
with its churn are given with each child.*

*The fee for fostering a son of the lowest order of chieftain is three cows; for the child of a king the fee is eighteen to thirty spotted cows. (The fee for a daughter is one-half milk cow more, for a daughter is more of a worry.) However, in certain cases, children may be fostered for affection, that is, no fee.*

*The son of a chieftain of a high grade shall be taught horsemanship, "brann" playing (a game like hurling), archery, chess-playing, and swimming. His daughter shall be taught sewing, cutting cloth for clothes, and embroidery.*

❦

*The son of a farmer shall learn to look after lambs,*
*calves, kids, and young pigs, as well as drying grain,*
*combing wool, and chopping firewood.  Whereas,*
*a daughter shall learn how to use the quern,*
*the kneading trough, and the sieve.*

*If a foster child is afflicted with the itch, or a serious disease,
it may be returned to its birth parents before marriage age.
(Or if the foster child commits a crime.)*

❦

*While in the care of foster parents the son of a king
of Erin shall wear satin and red clothes, own a
scabbard made of silver and a brooch of silver or gold,
have brass rings on his hurling stick, and be served
honey on his oatmeal.*

*The sons of the inferior classes of chieftains
shall wear black, yellow, or gray clothing, use scabbards
made of tin, and have butter on their oatmeal.*

❧

*The sons of the lowest class of chieftain shall
wear old clothes and eat salt butter.*

❧

*A fine shall be imposed upon foster parents who,
through carelessness and neglect, allow spikes and
spears, sticks and stones, or wicked cattle, to inflict
wounds upon their foster child.*

# Clergy

❦

*If* a monastery has wronged a member of the tribe,
or refuses to pay a debt, a piece of flexible willow shall
be tied on the monastery bell and at the foot of the altar,
to proclaim the misdeed.  No bells are to be rung, no
masses to be said until there is satisfaction.

❦

*If* a member of the clergy inflicts wounds on a member
of the tribe, or commits treachery, inhospitality, adultery,
or secret murder, he shall be deprived of his high rank in
society.  After paying the required fine and doing penance,
he shall return to his original rank, except a
bishop who must become a hermit.

*If a tribesman wounds a bishop, and the bishop's blood reaches the ground, the culprit shall hang for it.*

☙

*The bishop with one wife: if a tribesman suddenly grasps his hand or his clothes in supplication, or tries to deprive him of his bell, a fine shall be paid for insulting him.*

Crime

It is illegal for a bee to sting a passerby who has done
it no harm or anything illegal. If there are many
gardens in the area, and many bees, lots are to be cast
to discover from which garden the injury was done so
that the owner may be defined.

*If a suspect sleeps in heavily after a crime, this fact will cast doubt on his innocence. Or if he trembles, blushes, turns pale, or develops a thirst due to nervousness while being questioned.*

❦

*A shoe or a glove found near the scene of the crime or, in the case of a stolen animal, wet clothing or the discovery of bones or entrails near the suspect's house will be considered to be indirect evidence.*

# Distraint

❧

*Cattle may be impounded for two days for an evil word, one woman against another. That is, a wicked nickname, an evil word, a fault she has not, or an insulting word she does not deserve.*

❧

*If you do not hunt down pirates, horse-thieves, and wolves for your chieftain, or if you refuse to accompany him to the great assembly, your livestock shall be taken to the public animal pound for three days.*

*The professional satirist who bestows an evil-tongued nickname on a tribesperson, such as "foul-breath", "scabby-face" or "dung honour" shall have his cows, horses or gold jewellery seized for five days.*

❧

*If you cause a tree to wither through peeling its bark, or if you carry away an animal's covering (that is, the cloth which is about a mangy sheep), your livestock may be taken for five days.*

❧

*When cattle are taken to be impounded, if the journey is long they must be rested and fed at stations along the way.*

❦

*The keeper of the distraining-pound is obliged
to provide a pond for geese to swim in.
(And a cooling-pond for cattle.)*

❦

*For digging in a churchyard to steal from it, for making a
dam in a stream to take an excess of fish, or for stealing a
hunter's tent, your cattle will be taken to the animal pound
for three to ten days, depending on the circumstances.*

# Divorce

❦

*A husband may divorce his wife for:*
- *unfaithfulness;*
- *persistent thievery;*
- *inducing an abortion on herself;*
- *bringing shame on his honour; or*
- *smothering her child.*

❦

*Upon separation and divorce:
the woman who ploughs and reaps, feeds the young
of all cattle, and oversees the feeding of the working
men receives one-third of all the profits husband and
wife have accrued in the production of grain and bacon.*

❦

*The husband supported on the wife's property:*
*if he has helped with the ploughing, and has been a*
*good father to his children, he may take with him one-ninth*
*of the couple's increase in cows, hogs and grain.*

# Fines

✦

*If a tribesman breaks another tribesman's leg he must pay a fine and supply a horse for the victim to ride on.*

✦

*If the juggler at a fair juggles with pointed spears or sharpened knives, and injures a bystander, he pays a great fine. For this is a dangerous juggle.*
*The juggler of balls, however, should pay only a small fine (unless the victim was standing at a great distance), for this is deemed a safe juggle.*

*The fine for maiming a horse-boy is six young
heifers. For wounding a bishop the fine is forty-two cows.
Fines are doubled for malice aforethought.*

❦

*For a death maim, a great cow shall be paid to
the victim's family every night for nine nights.*

❦

*The fine for leaving a wounded man overnight
without nursing care is one cow.*

❧

*For injuring the man who goes with a thong in his cheek (the maker of leather shoes or wallets) the honour-fine, due his rank in society, is a fleece of wool, a ball of thread, and a hen without great delight. (That is, a hen that is not experiencing the great delight of laying or hatching eggs.)*

# Healing

❦

*The doctor may not keep his patients in his cow-house, his sheep-house, or his pig-house.*

❦

*The doctor need not take anyone into his house of healing whose death is probable.*

❦

*You may not drink ale while recuperating in the doctor's house unless the doctor directs it. If your visitor brings you food or drink forbidden by the doctor you must pay a fine.*

*An* unlimited amount of celery is allowed to patients
of every class, due to the abundance of its juice.
(It is for this above all that the herb garden is
made for the care of the sick.)

❦

*The* keeper of bees must share his honey with his
neighbours on all four sides, for the sick craving of
patients in their houses. (Sick craving is that for which
the invalid yearns at the depth of his sickness).

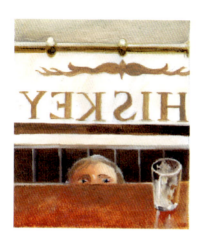

## Hospitality

❧

*All members of the tribe are required to offer hospitality*
*to strangers. The only exceptions are minor children,*
*madmen, and old people.*

*If anyone should take thy fatted sheep or hog, and a respectable company should arrive, and you have not food for them, the borrower shall pay it back on the same day, or on the morrow. If he or she does not, he shall pay you a blush-fine for your embarrassment.*

❦

*Whatever is cast ashore in a territory, whether a crew of shipwrecked people or a beached whale, the whole territory is bound to save it from the strand.*

*The* chieftain of the public hostel shall hold open house at all times for unexpected kings, bishops, poets, judges, and all other strangers. No fee shall be charged for bed or board, for the lands and cattle of every hostel are subsidised by the king.

❧

*The* public hostel shall be situated at the intersection of two roads. A man must be stationed at each road to make sure no traveller pass by without stopping to be entertained. A light shall be kept burning on the lawn to guide travellers from a distance.

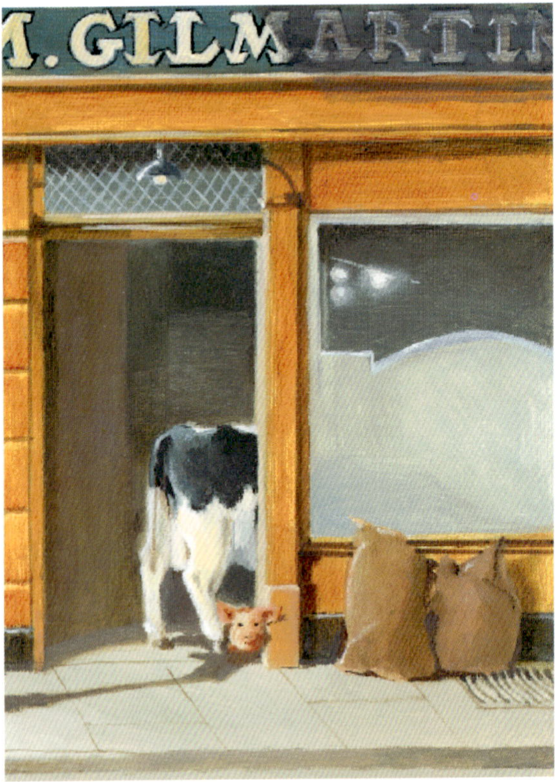
M.GILMARTI

*At all times the keeper of the public hostel shall have on hand: swine, sheep, and cattle in the field, fattened and ready for slaughter; pork, mutton, and beef, salted and hanging on hooks in the kitchen; and three boiled fleshes in the boiler, ready for instant serving.*

❧

*He should also have sixteen sacks of seeds in the ground, a brass pot into which a hog fits, and a lawn in which sheep stay without being driven off. (He also has a sack of malt to make ale, a sack of salt to cure his meats, and a sack of coal for the forge so his smith may repair his farm implements.)*

# Hunting and Fishing

❦

*In whatever place, it is a tribesman's right to spear a salmon seen near the top of the water. (But one thrust of the spear is all that is allowed.)*

❦

*If a hunted deer is brought down by dogs its belly goes to the owner of the land. The rest shall be divided among the hunters and the owners of dogs.*

❧

*For trapping a bird without permission the culprit must surrender two-thirds of its flesh and all of its feathers, and do forty days' penance.*

## Injuries

*It is safe for men to wear brooches upon their shoulders or their breasts providing they do not project too far beyond. (The same is true for women wearing brooches on their bosoms.) If they should, the case is to be adjudged by criminal law. For both men and women, projecting too far is wickedness.*

*If a slave accidentally kills or injures a passerby while chopping wood, neither he nor his master is liable for a fine or other punishment.*

❦

*The bond-maid is exempt from liability for injuring a bystander while she is arranging her baking flagstone and her kneading-trough, as long as she is at the work.*

# Kings

❦

*A king exercises not falsehood nor force nor oppressive might.*
*He is righteous towards all his people, both weak and strong.*

❦

*It is illegal for a king to raise pigs. (The royal swineherd*
*must live at a great distance from the palace.)*

❦

*A king of Ulster, if not accompanied by his retinue,*
*may not attack a wild boar in its den.*

*Three things that cause the overthrow of a king;
injustice, extortion, and kin-slaying.*

❧

*Five things expose the falsehood of a king: defeat
in battle, famine, the dryness of cows, a blight of
fruit, and scarcity of grain.*

❧

*A king may not travel alone, without witnesses, for
a lone woman may falsely swear her child upon the king.*

# Marriage

❧

*A woman is forbidden to marry one of these:*
- *a weaponless man, that is, he who is impotent;*
- *a man too gross, that is, his body is too fat for the work of satisfying her desire; or*
- *a man who tells their bed secrets.*

*(If before marriage she knew her husband to be weaponless they are both bound in law till hatred comes.)*

❧

*If a husband prefers the company of their servant boys to the company of his wife, she is free to divorce him.*

❧

*An "oinmit" ("buffoon") is a man who is matched with a bad wife by whom he is rendered deranged and unsteady.*

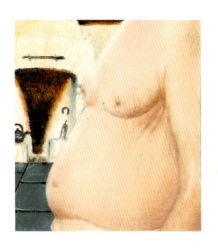

## Poets

🍂

*The poet historian has rank equal to the territorial king, unless he (the poet) speaks or teaches foolishly.*

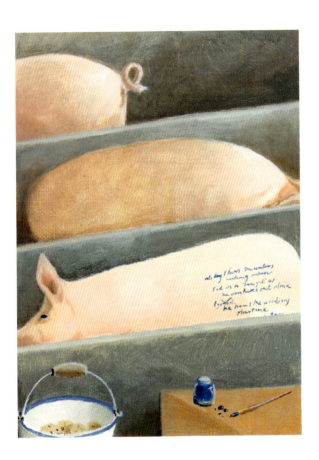

*A* poet praises his king or chieftain and satirises
their enemies, as the occasion requires.  If a poet
satirises a king unjustly he may cancel the
fine by composing a praise-poem.

❧

*P*oets are required to be free of the taint of theft
and killing, defamation and adultery - from
everything harmful to their learning.

❧

*W*hen an aging poet gives up his land to his foster child,
the student shall build him a small house on the property.
This house is known as tigh incis - the house of wisdom.

# Satire

❦

*The professional satirist, who snarls, barks, and bites like a dog, need not be paid a blush fine if you insult him, for he makes a trade of insulting others.*

❦

*The lawyer, who is paid to abuse others, is not entitled to claim damages when he is abused himself.*

❦

*The satirist who satirises a guiltless person will grow blisters on his own face. And then he will die.*

*It is illegal to satirise a tribesman for
a physical defect he was born with.*

❦

*If a blister appears on the cheek of a territorial king
because you have insulted or satirised him you owe
him thirty red-gold cows and a precious stone. (It is the
same as if he had been physically assaulted.)*

*The selfish man, who thinks only of his cows and his fields, and not of his fellow human beings, may be insulted without risking a blush fine.*

❧

*The face-reddening satire: it brings a blood-red face, as if the son of your mother or your sister had taken an illegitimate companion.*

❧

*The paling satire: it drains the countenance, like the face that becomes pale and white on account of theft or receiving stolen goods.*

# Sex

❦

*If a married woman is violated in an ale-house her assailant need not pay her compensation, for it was wrong to enter there without her husband for protection.*

❦

*A man's cattle shall be distrained for three days for violating a mad woman, incapacitating a woman for her work, bed witchcraft, neglecting co-habitation or carrying love charms (that is, charms intended to excite passion.)*

❦

*The woman who is violated in a town, but does not scream out until just after the man has escaped, is due no compensation. But if the violation occurs in a forest, he shall pay a fine.*

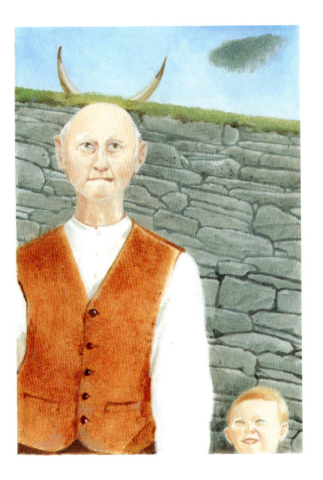

*To* every cuckold belongs his wife's child.

*(Unless the true father buys the child from him.)*

❦

*If* a child is born of a union forbidden by the
woman's family, the man alone is responsible for raising the
child. If the union has been forbidden by the man's family,
the woman will raise the child by herself.

# Victims and Sick Maintenance

❦

*If you wound a fellow tribes person you must take him or her to your own house, feed them according to the doctor's advice, provide the victim with medicine, and find a substitute to do his or her work while recuperating. You must also pay the doctor's fee.*

❦

*The victim's house of healing must not be filthy, nor may it be noisy, that is, it may not be near a roaring sea or a waterfall, a house where people are keening the dead, or a place where sheep are bleating in the spring.*

*A victim may not be taken to the house of an enemy.*

❦

*If a male victim is exceedingly lustful, or cannot separate from his women according to his great jealousy, he may bring his chief wife with him on sick maintenance.*

*It* is illegal to feed your victim horse-flesh while he is
under the doctor's care for it stirs up a storm in the
stomach and it increases bleeding for wounded heroes.

❦

*The* woman victim who goes on sick maintenance must
be accompanied by three female witnesses.
This is to protect her from the ardour of her host.

❦

*On* sick maintenance the cow-owning chieftain of
second class is entitled to porridge, butter on Sunday,
venison, sea grass, onions, and salt.

*There are three women who are not entitled to go on sick maintenance, and whose kinfolk must take care of them: the wanton woman who cares not with whom she sleeps; the female thief; and the sorceress who traffics in charms.*

❧

*In the case of a victim who may not go on sick maintenance the inflicter of the injury must pay a fine.*

# Women's Rights

❦

*Oxen that have become useless for ploughing shall not be sold without consultation between husband and wife.*

❦

*It is a more serious offence to kill a woman than to kill a man. The murderer shall have a hand and a foot cut off and he shall be put to death. His kin shall pay the price of 21 milk cows to her family.*

❦

# Glossary

*animals*

Like many early agricultural societies, the Irish considered their domestic animals working colleagues, members of the family and deserving of compassion. They also believed animals to be rational and responsible for their actions. In Europe, people put homicidal pigs, oxen, mules and other dangerous animals on public trial, and hanged the condemned beast in the village square or burned at the stake. In the case of a bug or a bird, the Catholic Church might excommunicate the evildoer.

*arbitration*

Arbitration was the backbone of Irish law. Penalties such as "distraint" were imposed so that wrongdoers and victims would be encouraged to submit to arbitration before a brehon (Irish jurist) rather than thrash out their differences between themselves.

*assemblies*

Recitation of old and new laws was the most important work of Irish assemblies but athletic games, entertainment and outdoor markets were part of the excitement.

*bed witchcraft*

To persuade a reluctant partner to bed down, a Greek would prepare a lovecharm of oysters, octopus or a mixture of orchids and goat's milk. A French lover might offer a bowl of truffle soup. The choice for an ancient Briton (sic) or Irishman boiled down to parsnips, turnips, leeks or cabbage.

*blush-fine*

Even to the ancient Greeks, the Celts were known as jealous of their honour. Vulnerability to ridicule and satire, even self-inflicted shame, could raise a blush, a blotch or a blister on an ancient Irish face. Anyone who caused a tribesman to be humiliated was required to pay a fine.

### brehon

Irish word for judge, advocate, arbitrator, law scholar, law professor.

### caste

Caste refers to hereditary careers or ranks in society. A person's rank in society was determined by the number of cows a lord or chieftain owned and by a person's occupation: king, poet, warrior, judge, blacksmith, goldsmith or other artisan, farmer, entertainer, etc down to slave.

### Celts

One of the four great barbarian tribes known to the ancients: Celtic, Scythian, Indian (Asian) and Libyan or Ethiopian. Though warlike, the Celts were known for their innovative uses of iron and admired for their intellectual ability. The names of some of the most sophisticated cities in Europe: London, Paris, Bonn and Vienna commemorate Celtic settlements.

### distraint/impoundment

Distraint was a method of penalising a lawbreaker and allowing the victim or creditor to seize a wrongdoer's property (livestock, jewellery or kitchen implements) after a certain number of days' notice.

### fines for injury and murder

A fine was calculated by a judge who added together a body fine (for injuring a particular part of the body) and the honour fine which represented a person's social rank.

*fosterage*

The custom of sending a child to a distant member of the tribe to be trained in the extended family's career (king, poet, warrior). Fosterage began at an early age, sometimes while the child was still being nursed. The child was returned to its birth family at marriage age: fourteen for girls, seventeen for boys.

*herb garden and healing*

Garlic, celery and honey made by bees buzzing about the herb garden were considered the most important foods and medication for an Irish patient.

*honour-price*

Each person in early Ireland society had an honour-price which determined certain privileges, such as the number of people in his entourage and fines to be paid to him or his family for injury or murder.

*Indo-European*

Indo-European refers to a language family and not a race. While living in Calcutta, the eighteenth century English Judge, Sir William Jones, noticed similarities between Sanskrit (India's formal language) and old Celtic and Germanic words. Other language scholars continued this research and discovered that all European language must have derived from one common language.

*keening*

Mourning for the dead which consisted in weeping and moaning, and incorporated praise and the genealogy of the deceased.

*kings*

In early Ireland, as many as 150 kings might have ruled at any one time.  Each king had about one thousand subjects.  A territorial king ruled over a tribe.  A provincial king ruled in each of the four provinces: Ulster, Leinster, Connacht and Munster.

*poet*

From the earliest times (first century BC), and before the development of a written Irish language, Irish poets were the keepers of Irish laws.

It was taboo to put the laws into writing and Irish poets were required to study for almost twenty years to memorise them.  They also memorised histories, genealogies and hundreds of tales of adventure and romance.  Prosody, the art of turning prose into almost mathematical metered verse formulae, was an especially important study which helped poets remember the laws with greater ease.

An Irish master poet held the same social rank as a king.

*satire*

The ancient Irish so dreaded having their honour impugned that they would give up their horses, their cattle or their favourite gold jewellery to avoid ridicule by a particularly cruel satirist.

*whale's eyebrow*

The "right whale" which cavorts in Irish waters, has an arched and hairy ridge over each eye, just like the human eye.

*withe-tie*

The withe-tie was a piece of flexible willow used for tying which was put on a tool such as a blacksmith's forge.  It was a humiliating announcement to the public that a member of the tribe owed an outstanding debt or had harmed a neighbour's property in some way.  The worker was on his honour to do no work until he had righted the wrong or paid the debt.